THE BOOK OF
BUNNY SUICIDES

VALEAS MUNDUM

ANDY RILEY HAS WRITTEN FOR BLACK BOOKS, TRIGGER HAPPY TV, SO GRAHAM NORTON AND SMACK THE PONY. HE HAS CO-WRITTEN THE BAFTA AWARD-WINNING ROBBIE THE REINDEER, THE RADIO FOUR PANEL GAME THE 99p CHALLENGE AND A DISNEY ANIMATION FEATURE, GNOMEO AND JULIET, TO BE RELEASED IN 2005. HE ALSO HAS A WEEKLY COMIC STRIP IN THE OBSERVER MAGAZINE.

THE BOOK OF
BUNNY SUICIDES

ANDY RILEY

Hodder & Stoughton

COPYRIGHT © 2003 BY ANDY RILEY
FIRST PUBLISHED IN GREAT BRITAIN IN 2003 BY HODDER AND STOUGHTON
A DIVISION OF HODDER HEADLINE
THE RIGHT OF ANDY RILEY TO BE IDENTIFIED AS THE AUTHOR OF THE WORK HAS
BEEN ASSERTED BY HIM IN ACCORDANCE WITH THE COPYRIGHT, DESIGNS
AND PATENTS ACT 1988.

A HODDER AND STOUGHTON HARDBACK

21

A CIP CATALOGUE RECORD FOR THIS TITLE IS AVAILABLE FROM THE BRITISH LIBRARY.
ISBN 978 0 340 82899 1

COVER AND PRELIMS DESIGN BY MARK ECOB
PRINTED AND BOUND IN GREAT BRITAIN BY WILLIAM CLOWES LTD, BECCLES, SUFFOLK
HODDER AND STOUGHTON
A DIVISION OF HODDER HEADLINE, 338 EUSTON ROAD, LONDON, NW1 3BH

WITH THANKS TO

KEVIN CECIL, ARTHUR MATHEWS

AND ALSO...

POLLY FABER, CAMILLA HORNBY,
KATY FOLLAIN + AMANDA SCHOENWALD

FOR POLLY

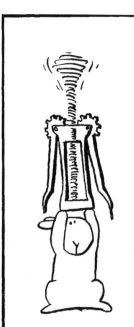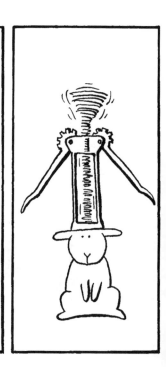

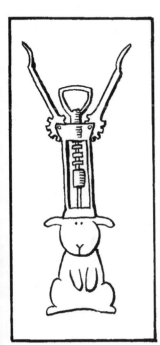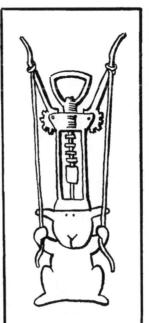

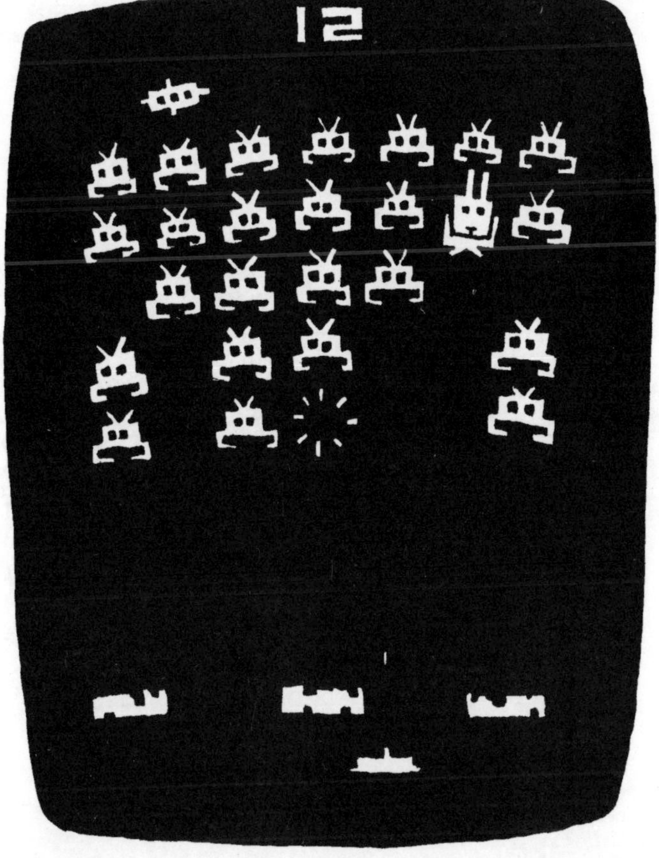
12

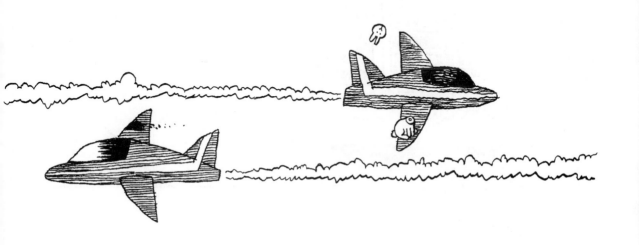

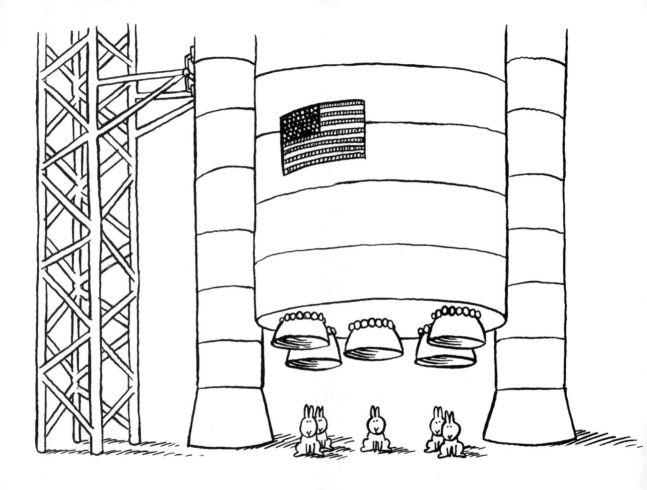

SHARKS

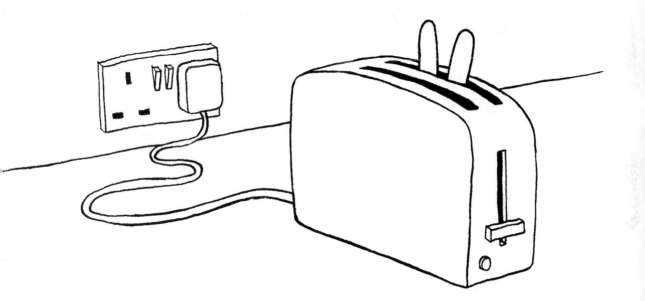

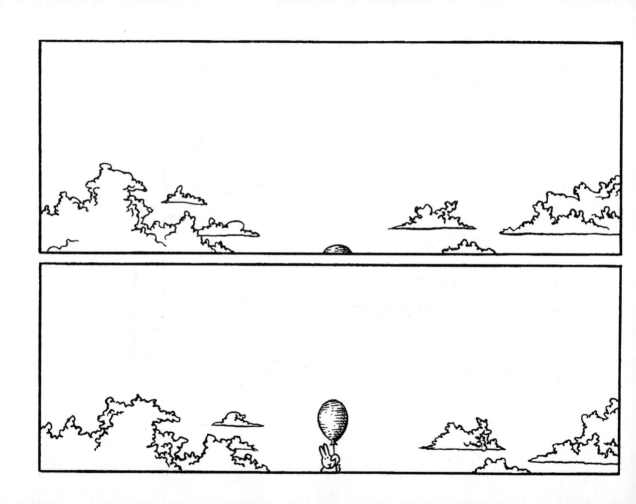

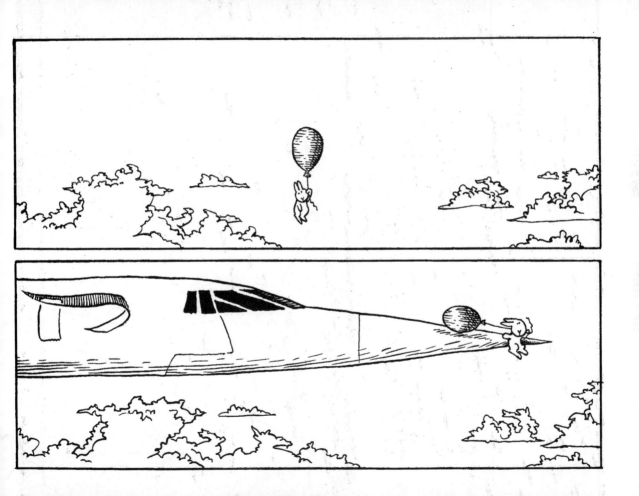

* TWO RABBITS JUGGLING CHISELS DURING A TOTAL ECLIPSE OF THE SUN

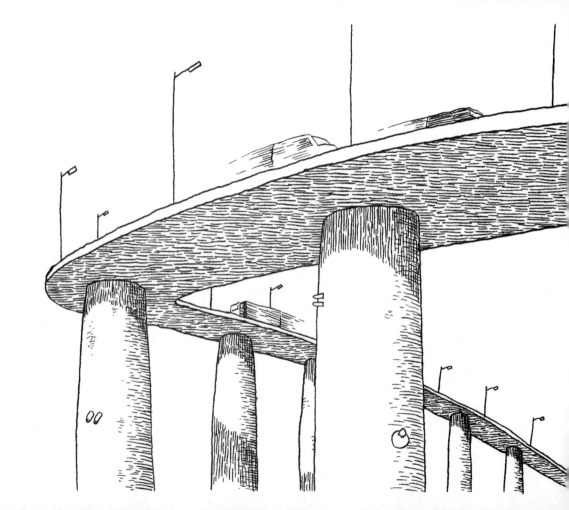

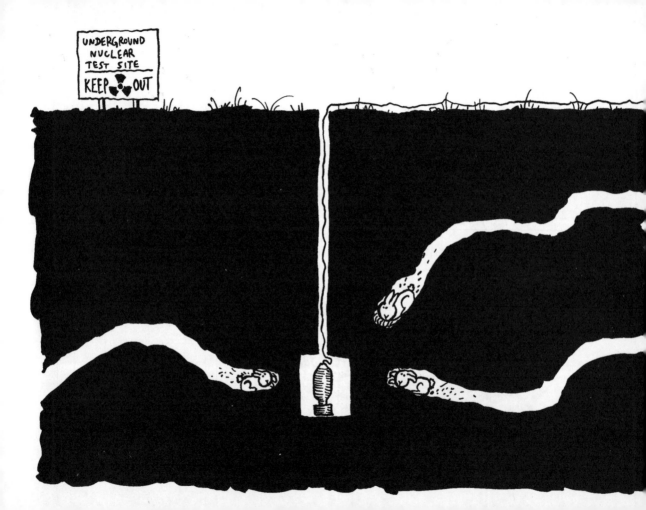

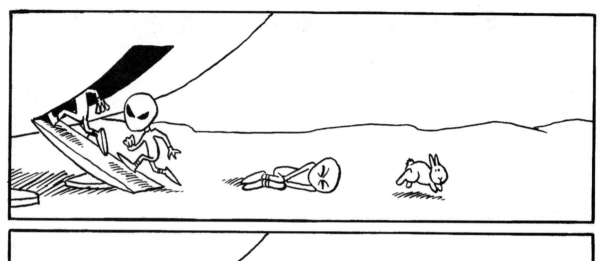
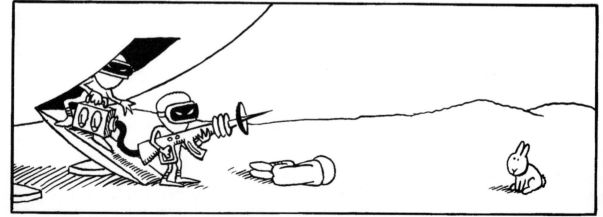

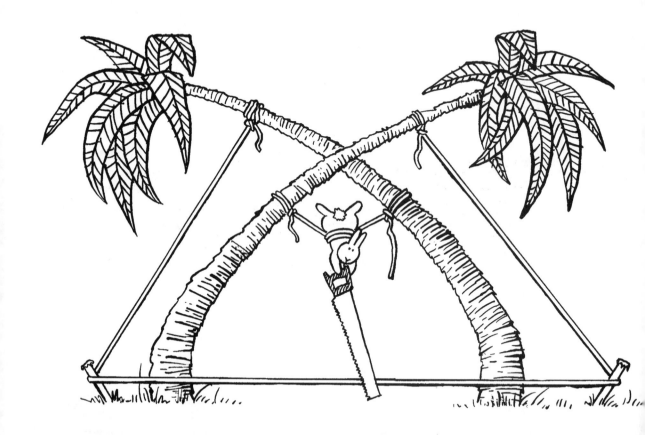

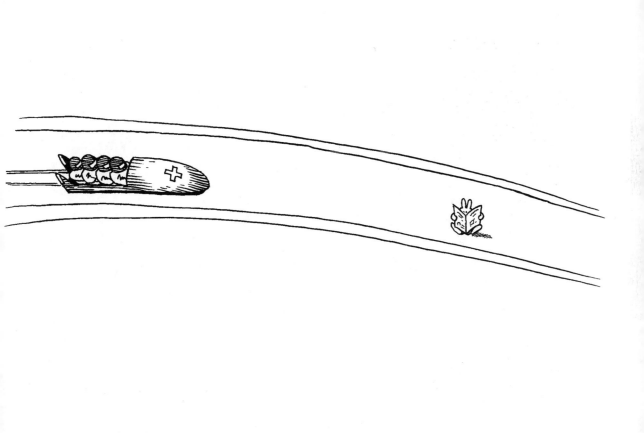

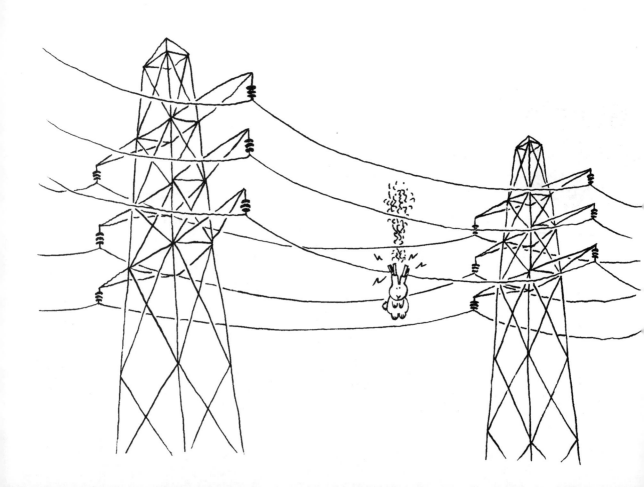

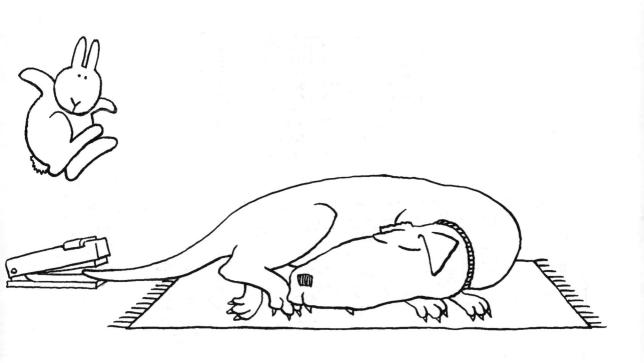